Introducti

C000253194

From the east the sharp profile of the Bl... frontier between lowland and highland easternmost ridge it is evident why this is th... Wales. To the east lie the fertile undulations o... ...ue English midlands. To the west, a succession of untamed ridges stretches to the western horizon. The Black Mountains are also the first and last mountains of Wales. The massif is the easternmost section of the Brecon Beacons National Park. The form of the Black Mountains can be pictured as an inverted hand. The northern edge is a spectacular escarpment looking out across the Wye Valley to Mid Wales. A series of tops adorn this scarp, and form the most impressive profile of the range. However these tops turn out to be just the terminal elevations of five main ridges stretching up to fifteen miles south, like fingers reaching out from knuckles. In between each ridge, long valleys drain the mountains.

In common with most of the National Park, the Black Mountains are chiefly laid on Old Red Sandstone. At lower levels there is an abundance of vegetation. Natural woodland includes alder, beech, hazel, oak and birch. Wild flowers grow in profusion in hedgerows that are centuries old. The slopes of the mountains are convex, rising steeply out of the valleys but gradually easing up to long ridges covered in heather, bilberry or bracken. There are a few small settlements but no real villages within the mountains. Abergavenny is the key town in the area, offering a wide range of facilities and bus/rail connections. Other centres include Talgarth, Crickhowell and Hay, best known for its panoply of second-hand bookshops.

The Black Mountains abound with historical interest and mystery. Iron Age forts were built from about 250BC and confirm the strategic importance of hilltops. **Walk 5** visits Dinas Castell, **Walks 16 & 17** Crug Hywel near Crickhowell and **Walk 14** Twyn-y-Gaer. The Normans made their mark on the region, often using more ancient fortified sites. Longtown Castle (**Walk 8**) and Tretower are examples (**Walk 10**). The influence of Christianity underpins the history of these hills. St David himself established a church on the site of Llanthony Priory (**Walks 3, 4 and 7**). Although the industrial revolution had little direct impact on most of the area, the hills to the south were in its melting pot. **Walks 18** and **19** visit the birthplace of iron making on the hillside above Blaenavon, now a World Heritage Centre.

Warning: Many of these walks cross open moorland, and on these mountain precautions should always be taken. Ensure that you are appropriately dressed (*with extra clothing in your rucksac even in summer*), have good walking boots, a compass and basic emergency equipment. And don't forget to take some food and drink.

RHOS DIRION FROM RHOS FACH

DESCRIPTION A 5½-mile circular walk around the Black Mountains' dramatic northern escarpment. An ancient road across the range offers a clear line of ascent. The effort is rewarded with outstanding views along an easy traverse of the ridge. The return route follows a lovely descent through bracken and gorse along the base of the mountains' steep buttresses.

START Rhos Fach Common. SO 187334.

DIRECTIONS Rhos Fach Common lies about two miles east of Talgarth along a minor road. The road starts in the centre of the town, opposite the Coop, and passes an old hospital before gaining a shelf of land below the Black Mountains escarpment. Rhos Fach Common is open land and it is easy to leave a car on firm grass at the side of the road. *This walk includes high level moorland. You should take appropriate equipment, including navigation aids.*

1 FOLLOW A WIDE GRASSY TRACK eastwards heading towards the hillside. *This is actually an old road traversing the Black Mountains via the Grwyne Fawr valley on the other side of the escarpment. Hence the sign at the beginning banning all vehicles except 'motorcycles with or without sidecars'. You may well feel that a ride in a sidecar over this terrain would be an experience worth missing! The environment is largely one of rough grassland but there are signs of ancient agriculture and the remains of some strip fields in the area.* Follow the track and cross a stile next to a conifer plantation. Continue on the track as it veers left through bracken and gorse to follow the line of a wire fence up the hillside. The fence remains our companion until we gain the summit plateau, though it is not marked on OS maps. The track becomes more eroded and less grassy but is a steady ascent, offering widening views over Talgarth and beyond to the Wye Valley. After a while it curves right to climb up the side of the deep, rocky defile of Cwm Cwnstab. After a double bend in the track, the gradient eases before a final ascent to the top of the escarpment.

2 As you reach the head of the cwm, the path veers left following the line of the fence. About 100 yards further, GO LEFT through a gate in the fence leaving the old track which continues across the moor towards Grwyne Fawr reservoir. *The new path ascends gently across grassy terrain, which is intermittently soggy. There are views south down the Grwyne Fawr valley and on to Pen y Gadair Fawr and Waun Fach. Soon views open out northwards over the Wye Valley.*

3 The summit of the walk is reached at a trig point on Rhos Dirion, marking a height of 713m. *This is also the highest point on the Black Mountains' impressive northern escarpment, though apart from this topographical detail the summit itself is little more than a featureless grassy swelling on the edge of the moor. The same certainly cannot be said of the view from here, which includes a wide swathe of Mid Wales extending from Carmarthen Fan and the Brecon Beacons in the west to Radnor Forest in the north.* From here, the route continues along the edge of the escarpment, now following a gentle but steady descent until the path reaches the head of a deep defile at Rhiw y Fan. Follow the path carefully around this as it curves slightly to the left. About 400 yards further on reach a junction. It is clear on the ground, but would be easy to miss if concentration lapses, so watch out. (If you want to extend the walk slightly and climb to the top of Twmpa, continue forward. The summit lies about 700 yards ahead up a gentle climb. Retrace your steps to this point to rejoin the circuit.)

4 At the junction, take the track that SLANTS LEFTWARDS descending below the escarpment. This is a bridleway that has crossed the mountains from the Vale of Ewyas and now drops gently down the northern slopes of the range. After another 400 yards, the track turns back sharply to the left and becomes a grassy passageway through ferns. Ahead in the distance lie the peaks of the Brecon Beacons. *To the left you can now see the escarpment from below, with the impressive exposed red sandstone strata giving the Black Mountains their distinctive profile.* Continue to follow the line of this path, ignoring turn offs to the right (the line of the bridleway is one of these turn-offs). A little further on, just above a reedy gully, the path curves to the right and descends gently to join a tarmac lane just by a ford.

5 TURN LEFT here and follow the lane as it weaves through bracken and then turns sharp right over a stream. It continues through a grove of alder trees to reach a gate. Pass through the gate and continue along the road, descending to the farmhouse at Blaenau-isaf. The road climbs from the house

and soon reaches a gate giving access to open land.

6 Go through the gate, then BEAR LEFT, leaving the road to follow a path across the common land, Rhos Fawr. Maintain this direction across the heath, with Pen y Fan, the highest peak of the Beacons, directly ahead in the distance. Pass a small pond and soon pick up the line of a fence, following this on its right hand side. The path drops into a small valley and picks up a track. Follow this left, soon leading through a gate and crossing a stream. The track becomes a sunken lane, which can be muddy but this shortly emerges back on to open heath land. This is now Rhos Fach. Continue across a stony track, keeping to the grassy path in line with the fence. This brings you back to the starting point.

WALK 2

TWMPA, NANT BWCH & DARREN LWYD

DESCRIPTION This 6 mile walk starts in the idyllic hamlet of Capel-y-ffin, nestling in the upper reaches of the Honddu valley. An initial steep climb up the ridge of Darren Lwyd is rewarded with splendid views and much gentler walking to the summit of Twmpa on the northern escarpment of the Black Mountains. The return route follows the charming valley of Nant Bwch until it joins the Honddu back at Capel-y-ffin. High level sections require appropriate precautions

START Capel-y-ffin. SO 255314. An alternative start is at Gospel Pass GR SO 236351.

DIRECTIONS The village is situated on the minor road between Hay and Abergavenny. This joins the A465 at Llanfihangel Crucorney. It is a scenic but narrow route crossing the Gospel Pass at 538 metres above sea level. Note that parking is very limited in Capel-y-ffin. There are a few spaces on the verges or where the lane widens, but these can be taken quickly at weekends. The alternative start at Gospel Pass offers easier parking. There is a car park at the side of the road here, just south of its highest point. A clear track leads from the summit of the road, following the escarpment to the summit of Twmpa. Then follow the instructions from Point **2.** This adds just over a mile to the total distance.

*C*apel-y-ffin lies near the head of the Honddu valley, at the river's confluence with Nant Bwch. Its name means 'Chapel of the Boundary', situated in the far north of Monmouthshire, close to its border with Brecknock, now Powys. Its peaceful setting, deep in a fertile, wooded valley has attracted many people. A Roman Catholic priest, Father Ignatius, founded a monastery here in 1869. In 1924 the buildings were taken over by Eric Gill who established a self-sufficient religious community. He worked as a sculptor and calligrapher, devising 11 new fonts, the best known of which is Gill Sans (one of the typefaces in this book). 'The Monastery' can still be seen on the side of the hill to the west of the village, though there is no public access.

From the bridge follow the road northwards towards Hay, passing the white painted church on your right. *This is St Mary's, part of the Church in Wales. It was built in 1762 and includes an eighteenth century pulpit and a medieval font. It is one of the smallest churches in Wales, measuring 25 feet by 12 feet.* In about 300 yards, by a sign to the Grange Trekking Centre, a public footpath sign indicates a route LEFT over a stile and then through a gate. This path ascends a field towards a house. The steep ridge of Darren Lwyd looms up before you. At the top of the field cross a stile and then pass between the house and a converted barn. The right of way goes straight on, through a clear gap in the hedge, and then to a gate leading to open country. A steep stony path begins the assault of Darren Lwyd, following the line of a fence. Where the fence veers to the left, by an ash tree, TURN SHARP RIGHT and follow a narrow path ascending through the bracken. Keep to this narrow but clear path as it maintains this line, climbing diagonally across the side of the hill, ignoring any tracks that cross it. After a while, above the buildings of Trwyn-tal below you, the path swings sharply left and continues its diagonal ascent in the opposite direction. Soon you gain the nape of the ridge and the path turns right to climb directly up to a cairn on the skyline. *It's not quite the top, but the worst is over, and you can afford to pause and enjoy the views back over Capel-y-ffin and the Vale of Ewyas. Notice the clear U-shape of the valley, carved not by the River Honddu alone, but also by glacial erosion.* A much gentler ascent now lies ahead as the path crowns the ridge of Darren Lwyd. The valley road can be seen snaking up towards the Gospel Pass and, on the left, there are views across Nant Bwch to the highest land of the Black Mountains. The path keeps more or less to the crest of the ridge and, where the ridge broadens, keeps ahead across the moor to gain the summit of Twmpa, where the ground abruptly falls away with the stream near a waterfall, an idyllic place to picnic. A gate leads from the open country on to a surfaced lane, passing the farmhouse of Blaen-bwch. It soon descends through woods. This is a very quiet lane and a pleasure to walk. Hedges provide a fertile habitat for wild flowers such as the abundant Herb Robert. The lane leads gently down to Capel-y-ffin passing a riding centre as you enter the hamlet.

There are actually two chapels at Capel-y-ffin. The whitewashed building of the Church

to the Wye Valley. *Twmpa's alias, Lord Hereford's Knob, attracts speculation and innuendo, but there seems to be no real knowledge of the origin of this intriguing English nomenclature. Enjoy the truly panoramic views, this time northwards across the Wye Valley to Radnor Forest and beyond. (If you started the walk at Gospel Pass, turn right and retrace your steps down to the road).*

2 At the summit cairn, TURN LEFT and follow the path down from the summit. Where paths diverge, keep to the route nearest to the edge of the escarpment, as this will aid navigation.

3 A stony track leads sharply down to the right to drop down diagonally from the ridge. In the opposite direction a grassy path crosses the moor. TURN LEFT to follow this. It soon descends gently towards the valley of Nant Bwch, crossing the infant stream and keeping to the left hand bank. The stream drops more steeply than the path, so soon you have a pleasant view down the increasingly vertiginous banks clothed with ferns, bilberries and heather. *The path is reunited*

in Wales stands next to the road by the bridge. Its tiny gallery offers an aerial view of the church and the pulpit dates from 1786. The Baptist chapel lies a short way along the lane behind and was built in 1737. Above Capel-y-ffin, the road narrows and begins to climb the upper reaches of the Honddu valley to the Gospel Pass, an alternative start to **Walk 2**. *The pass stands at 1778 feet above sea level, making this road the second highest in Wales.*

THE VALE OF EYWAS

DESCRIPTION A 4½-mile circuit of the Vale of Ewyas. An ascent up the attractive valley of Cwm Bwchel leads to a cairn at Bal-Bach, marking the summit of a mountain pass. An old bridleway contours the side of the ridge, offering views across Llanthony and its historic ruins, before descending to the river. The return journey travels along the bottom of the valley, making use of paths and little used lanes. The woods and hedgerows create their own natural haven for wild life and plants.

START Llanthony Priory. GR SO 289278

DIRECTIONS A minor road off the A465 Abergavenny to Hereford trunk road reaches Llanthony Priory. Turn off the main road at Llanfihangel Crucorney and follow the signposts to Llanthony. From the north this minor road starts at Hay and climbs over the Gospel Pass. There is a car park at Llanthony Priory. There are also toilets here and a pub nearby offers refreshments, though its opening hours can be intermittent.

*L*lanthony Priory lies in a wild and beautiful setting, cocooned among the trees and hedgerows of the Vale of Eywas, immediately below the steep bracken clad ridge. This rises up to the English border, less than a mile away. Christian worship first took place here over 1400 years ago when St David himself founded a chapel. The present remains date from the Norman period, when William de Lacy established a priory in about 1118. Later that century, Gerald of Wales visited Llanthony as part of his tour of Wales, recruiting soldiers for the Crusades. He commented it was situated among 'barbarous people'. The priory never really flourished. By the time of the dissolution of the monasteries in 1536, there were just four monks and the site was sold for less than £200. None of this detracts from its place as one of the best medieval buildings in Wales. It certainly occupies a classic position, and was inevitably painted by Turner on a visit in the nineteenth century.

1 Follow the priory access road back to the lane along the valley. To your left, on the opposite side of the lane, is a footpath sign to Bal-Bach. FOLLOW THE FOOTPATH, which goes to the right of the phone box, just in front of Mill House. Cross the River Honddu on a footbridge. On the far side of the bridge, turn right and cross a stile heading for Bal-Bach. Soon another stile leads into a muddy green lane. Thankfully cross over this, passing through a gate on the opposite side, to follow the signpost for Cwm Bwchel. Marker posts now lead you up through fields, crossing stiles and a small stream. The route then follows the right hand side of the stream up past the farm buildings at Cwm Bwchel to gain the open mountainside by a stile. Climb steadily up the side of the little valley with thorn trees and bracken giving colour and interest, with the sound of the stream accompanying you all the way. Views of the priory and its surroundings offer a photogenic rear view you as you gain height. As it emerges from the cwm, the path continues to climb through wilder, open country. It is now less steep and an engineered route spares you the bracken and squelchy peat.

2 At the cairn at Bal-Bach, TURN RIGHT to follow a broad track. After about 150 yards leave this – it is the line of Walk 4 up to Bal-Mawr. Instead FORK RIGHT along a grassy track that contours around the side of the hill. The route is a pleasant traverse through bracken and bilberries and you can enjoy views across the Honddu Valley to the Hatterrall Ridge and the border with England on the opposite side. The path is level at first and then descends gently. As it rounds the valley of Nant-y-Carnau, it drops more steeply. Eventually you come to a gate and pass through this into some trees. There is an old ruined building down to the right. Just beyond this, TURN RIGHT and go down hill, following the left hand edge of the field towards the farm buildings. Just before these, a signpost points on down to the Valley Road through a small, rough field. Cross this patch of land, which can be overgrown and awkward. It's less than 100 yards down to a gate leading to the farm access road. This track leads gently and directly to the valley road.

3 TURN LEFT and follow it for about 300 yards. Then TURN RIGHT along a no through road, signposted to a trekking centre. Cross the bridge over the river. *This River Honddu is one of two identically named watercourses in the area. Rising above Capel-y-ffin this one flows southeast through the Vale of Ewyas through Llanthony to Llanfihangel Crucorney. Here it is forced to reverse its intended direction and flow northwards to join the Monnow at Pandy, a few miles north of Abergavenny. The Monnow loops around northern Gwent to join at the Wye at Monmouth. The other Honddu drains Mynydd Eppynt, north of Brecon,*

and joins the Usk right in the centre of the town. Soon after the bridge the lane curves to the left but you TURN SHARP RIGHT through a gate onto a track. This leads to another surfaced cul-de-sac, which brings you back to Llanthony.

Tafalog Bridge

Sychtre **3**

Nant-y-carnau

Vale of Ewyas

Nantygwyddel

Broadley

Afon Honddu

Llanthony Priory

Pub **P** **START**

Llanthony

Troed-rhiw-mon

0   Miles   ½

N

Cwm Bwchel

Walk 4

Bal-Bach

2

Llanthony Priory

WALK 4

CHWAREL-Y-FAN & OFFA'S DYKE PATH

DESCRIPTION A 9-mile walk exploring the upper reaches of the Vale of Eywas. Starting at the historic ruins of Llanthony Priory, the route ascends the delightful side valley of Cwm Bwchel to gain the Ffawyddog ridge. The ridge provides an airy and almost level traverse above the valley with extensive views across the whole of the Black Mountains. After the highest point, Chwarel-y-Fan, there is a descent to the isolated hamlet of Capel-y-ffin. The return leg entails a steep climb up the opposite ridge, followed by a stride along the border following Offa's Dyke Path (though not the dyke itself). The final descent offers classic views of the photogenic priory ruins. *This walk includes high level moorland. You should take appropriate equipment, including navigation aids.*
START Llanthony Priory. SO 289278.
DIRECTIONS See **Walk 3**.

1 The first part of the route follows **Walk 3** as far as Bal-Bach (instruction **1**). For historical background to Llanthony see **Walk 3**.

2 A cairn marks the summit of the path. TURN RIGHT here to follow a broad track up the summit of Bal-Mawr, which is marked by a trig point. Continue beyond the summit on a clear path along the airy Ffawyddog ridge. *Enjoy views right over the Vale of Ewyas with Llanthony now far below. The Hatterrall ridge on the far side of the valley marks the border with England, and also the line of Offa's Dyke long distance footpath. Leftwards, your eye is drawn across the afforested valley of the Grwyne Fawr to Pen y Gadair Fawr and Waun Fach, the highest of the Black Mountain summits beyond.* The ridge provides a steady and easy walk, with slight undulations at Bwlch Isaf and Bwlch Bach before making a slight ascent to the top of Chwarel-y-Fan, marked by a large cairn at over 670 metres. Gently descend from the summit. In just over ½ mile reach a cairn marking a fork in the path.

3 This junction is known as the Blacksmith's Anvil. TAKE THE RIGHT FORK. The path descends gently at first, and then becomes more steep and rocky as it passes over the side of the ridge. Capel-y-ffin can now be seen below, with the ruins of the monastery clearly visible. Reach a grassy shelf, cross a stream and descend to the left of a conifer wood on an increasingly eroded track. The route emerges on to a lane by a trekking centre. TURN RIGHT, soon reaching the road junction and bridge at Capel-y-ffin. *See* **Walk 2** *for more information about this hamlet.*

4 Cross the river and GO THROUGH THE GATE TO THE RIGHT of the white painted church. Follow the lane as it crosses a footbridge, passes a second chapel and goes through another gate. The path goes to the left of the house and through a further gate. It then crosses a number of fields, contouring along the base of the steep ridge to your left, and easily crossing small watercourses that drain the hillside. After a while the lane becomes surfaced and you pass through a couple more gates. Immediately after the second gate, you leave the lane and turn SHARP LEFT over a stile at a signpost to 'The Hill' and 'Offa's Dyke'. Yellow waymarks indicate the route RIGHT towards the farm and then steeply LEFT straight up the hillside. A stile leads into some beech and ash woodland and the path continues relentlessly up hill. At the top of the wood, a stile leads to open countryside and the path turns RIGHT for a brief level section. Shortly, the path turns back to the LEFT renewing its resolve to conquer the ridge and reach the border on the top. The path is steep as it snakes its way through the bracken, which can be quite high in late summer, but the way is clear enough. Eventually the convex slope eases and the ferns give way to grass, clues that your labour is nearly complete.

5 The path meets a major track on the crest of the ridge. If you've kept to the official route, you should join it at a pile of stones, but, even if you've strayed a bit, you will not miss the track. TURN RIGHT and follow it south, enjoying an extensive panorama over a wide area. *This is Offa's Dyke Long Distance Footpath on its way from Chepstow to Prestatyn. This ridge makes a splendid course for the footpath. It is easy to see why the border runs here, perhaps more than anywhere else along its length. To the west lie tiers of mountains parading into the interior of Wales, wild, rugged and confusing to an invader. To the east, the fertile fields of Herefordshire lead to the English Midlands, the outlines of the Malverns and Cotswolds decorating the horizon.* You pass a trig point part the way along this featureless ridge.

6 A sign to Llanthony on a stone slab marks the point where the path to the valley leaves the ridge. TURN RIGHT here. The descent is gentle at first but soon becomes much steeper as the ruins of the priory come into view over the brow of the hill. Although the gradient is serious, the path is clear and easy to negotiate and eventually a stile leads off the open access land. Descend the field beyond it and then cross two more stiles with a small copse between them. More fields lead gently down towards the historic walls of the priory and the starting point.

Y GRIB
& WAUN FACH

DESCRIPTION The highest castle in Wales and England and the highest point in the Black Mountains are both visited on this 7-mile expedition. A short but steep climb leads to Dinas Castell, which commands the top of the Rhiangoll valley, a strategic pass through the mountains between Mid and South Wales. From here an appealing walk up the switchback ridge of Y Grib leads to the summit plateau. This commands stunning views from the Cotswolds to Carmarthenshire, and swells gently to the top of Waun Fach. The return route descends the ridge of Pen Trumau and turns down an old route traversing the fell side into the valley below. *The walk includes remote moorland and mountain terrain, which require proper clothing and equipment as well as competent use of navigation aids in misty weather.* **Take a compass.**

START Castle Inn, Pengenffordd SO 174297.

DIRECTIONS The Castle Inn is situated just south of the highest point on the A479 between Abergavenny and Talgarth. There is a large pub car park on the southbound side of the road, immediately north of the Castle Inn. Non-patrons are asked to pay £1 for parking.

1 From the northern end of the car park, follow the sign to Castell Dinas leading down some steps to a bridleway. TURN RIGHT along this lane for 50 yards and then cross a stile on the LEFT. Follow the side of the field to another stile, crossing this and a small stream. A steep ascent then faces you up to the top of Castell Dinas. Climb two fields, keeping the fence on your left. A third field, this time with the fence on your right brings you to the castle site.

2 Reaching the summit ridge, you TURN LEFT and the path weaves its way through the remains of the castle, which consists mainly of some mounds. *The original fort dates from the Iron Age and there was probably a Welsh stronghold here. The site commands the top of the Rhiangoll valley,*

a key pass between the Usk and Wye valleys. The Normans made use of the position in the twelfth century. Some of their ditches and ramparts still evident today, although little remains of any masonry. At the end of the castle site, the path descends, crossing a defensive ditch and passing an old well, until it reaches the saddle. Cross the stile, which gives access to the open mountainside. The beginning of the Dragon's Back ridge (or Y Grib) now lies directly before you. Avoid the tracks either side of the ridge and take the grassy path more or less up the centre as it weaves its way through bracken. A small wind shelter marks the top of the first part of the 'Dragon's Back'. Descend a little way to the next col and continue like this on up the ridge, keeping where possible to the crest for greatest effect, though alternative routes sometimes lurch slightly to the side. *Gliders may accompany you from the nearby flying club as they swoop up above the highest land and use the thermal currents to return to the airfield.*

3 At the top of a rock section a significant cairn marks the top of Y Grib and the beginning of more open mountain country. Care is now needed to find the right route. In clear weather there will be no problem. You are simple aiming for the slight elevation on the ridge in front of you, which is Pen y Manllwyn and it doesn't really matter which course you follow to get there. However, in misty weather navigation will be important. About 50 yards after the cairn, there is a faint bifurcation in the path, which is easy to miss. The more prominent left hand fork leads around the edge of the steepest slopes to Y Das. However, our route takes the RIGHT HAND FORK on a bearing of 90 degrees. A small pile of stones about 10 yards after the junction confirms your choice and the path heads across the shoulder of land, with some wet patches in places. Once on the path, it's clear enough to follow and after a while it ascends more steeply. The path emerges on to the ridge track just north of Pen y Manllwyn, though short cuts may lead you straight to its 'summit', a slight soggy swelling.

4 TURN RIGHT and and follow the wide and boggy 'path' along the broad ridge, negotiating peaty channels from time to time. The route is generally level until the short final

ascent to the summit of Waun Fach. *This is the highest point in the Black Mountains at 810 metres, but has little to commend it as a summit. A vast mire of black peat surrounds a lump of concrete. Even the OS has turned its back on Waun Fach, preferring to grace other landmarks for triangulation surveys. However, the views are more than adequate compensation for Waun Fach's other inadequacies. Eastwards the panorama stretches across the rest of the Black Mountains to the Clee Hills in Shropshire and the Cotswolds in Gloucestershire; southwards across the Bristol Channel to distant Exmoor; westwards far across Wales to Carmarthen Fan and beyond.*

5 At the summit, TURN RIGHT and follow a course west-south-west (240 degrees). You will need a compass in poor visibility, as the path is not evident from the peaty quagmire of the summit. However, it becomes clear after a few yards and from then on you should have no route finding problems. A steady but easy descent leads along the ridge to Pen Trumau, with views back to Y Grib and Dinas Castell to your right. Follow the broad crest of the ridge as it turns in a more southerly direction. A steeper and rockier section leads to a narrow saddle of land at the col between Waun Fach and Mynydd Llysiau

6 A cairn marks the junction of paths at this idyllic mountain pass. Walks 15 and 17 link here. Our route requires you to TURN SHARP RIGHT. The track slants down across the hillside and in about 200 yards be careful to follow the main path as it BEARS LEFT to descend directly down the mountain. (Avoid the contouring path ahead). The gradient steepens and the path becomes stonier as the Rhiangoll valley comes fully into view below. *Thorn trees and bracken now accompany you on a charming terrace path.* A series of gates herald entry into enclosed land and a fenced lane leads down to a tarmac side road. TURN RIGHT and in 50 yards BEAR LEFT. The lane drops down to cross the Rhiangoll and passes a riding centre. 300 yards after the riding centre, the lane bends sharply back to the left. At this point, carry STRAIGHT AHEAD on to a rather muddy track. Cross a small ford and carry on up the bridleway as it ascends gently, parallel to the main road. It soon leads back to the steps, which return you to the car park and the start of the walk.

WALK 6

THE VALLEY OF THE GRWYNE FAWR

DESCRIPTION The story of a saint and a murderer endow this walk with mystery and heritage from the mists of time. The 5-mile circuit of the middle reaches of the Grwyne Fawr valley starts along good tracks through Mynydd Du forest. Once in open country a traverse of the lower slopes of Crug Mawr offers a panorama across the valley. Pause at Patrishow, an ancient church perched on an isolated hillside and dedicated to St Issui. Pilgrims still visit the well of this early Celtic saint, hidden in trees just below the church. The return route crosses the river and follows its eastern side, with good views back across the Grwyne Fawr.

START Car park at Pont Cadwgan accessed by a bridge across the river from the valley road. SO 267252.

DIRECTIONS The valley road is a cul-de-sac, which starts at the crossroads at Forest Coalpit. It follows the Grwyne Fawr river northwards deep into the heart of the Black Mountains. Forest Coalpit can be accessed by narrow lanes from Crickhowell or by leaving the A465 at Llanfihangel Crucorney, four miles north of Abergavenny.

I Go back to the car park entrance and cross the road. Follow a forestry road slanting uphill through the trees. After about half a mile come to a junction of forest roads and BEAR LEFT, following a sign to Ffordd-las-fawr. Continue on this level track through the woods. *Enjoy the variety of trees here, with a range of deciduous species surviving the onward march of the ubiquitous conifer.* Continue STRAIGHT ON at another junction of bridleways and continue with the track as it curves over a stream and passes between derelict buildings at Ffordd-las fawr. *This valley used to be much more populous than today. Until the nineteenth century over 30 farmsteads provided a livelihood for its inhabitants.* At the far end of the buildings

TURN LEFT. In 150 yards keep straight on at a junction of bridleways, continuing on the level path, now narrower.

2 Soon a gate marks the end of the forest and leads immediately to a mountain stream. Fording this may be difficult if it is in full spate after heavy rain. However, there is an easier step across a few yards upstream. On the other side of the stream FOLLOW THE BRIDLEWAY LEFT up the side of the hill. It follows the wall marking the boundary of open land and gradually curves round to become parallel to the Grwyne Fawr valley. At the end of the open countryside, pass two gates and a sheepfold on to a green lane between two fences. This soon leads to a tarmac lane. TURN RIGHT and descend steeply to the tiny church at Patrishow. You can enter the churchyard by a stile or the lych gate. *There is evidence that a church may have been established here before the time of William the Conqueror and the inscription on the font has been dated to about 1055. According to legend, it was financed by an outsider as an offering of thanks for a cure from leprosy. The nave may be Norman and the screen and rood loft date from around 1400. The road continues down to a bridge. Just beside this is St Issui's Well (Ffynnon Ishow). This early Christian priest lived near the well and offered hospitality to travellers. He was murdered by one such itinerant and his well has since been a site of Celtic pilgrimage for centuries. The small spring, framed by stone, lies down a few steps amidst the trees, usually adorned with flowers or greenery.*

3 From the well, turn back towards the church but immediately TURN RIGHT over a stile. The path follows the bottom of the field below the church to reach another stile. This gives access to a lane. Pass to the right of a white farmhouse and continue down to the valley road. TURN LEFT and walk along the road carefully for about 300 yards. At a sign to Tabernacle Chapel BEAR RIGHT down the lane, which curves right to cross the river. You pass the Tabernacle Baptist chapel to your left. An inscription dates this to 1837. Follow the lane around to track a gate bars your way into a riverside meadow. Follow the path to the RIGHT of the fence to avoid this. You rejoin the track at the other end of the meadow. It now follows the river and leads onto a concrete track that then ascends to a farmhouse. Go through the gate onto the metalled lane following it down to the bridge and the valley road by a red phone box.

5 TURN RIGHT along the road. You can simply follow the road for about a mile back to the start. It's quiet and wide enough to avoid close encounters with any traffic there is. If you don't like road walking, BEAR LEFT in 100 yards to follow a footpath sign. You climb back into the woods to join the forest road that was our outward route. TURN RIGHT and descend back to the car park. *The road along the valley was only completed in 1912 as part of a reservoir construction project. The Grwyne Fawr Reservoir at the head of the valley was completed in 1928. It was built to provide water for the area around Abertillery in the Western Valley of Monmouthshire. A temporary town, Blaen-y-cwm, was built to house the workers. You can visit the reservoir by continuing along the valley road to its terminus where another car park is provided.*

the LEFT as it climbs the side of the valley. Just past the gate take the upper track signposted to Upper House, passing above Ty Mawr farmhouse.

4 *From Ty Mawr, the path leading up sharply to the right leads to Twyn-y-Gaer. It links with point 5 on* **Walk 14** *if you want to extend the walk to visit the ancient fort.* To continue with this walk, ignore the turning and ascend the lane ahead to Upper House. Here, ignore another right hand turn to 'The Hill', instead carry STRAIGHT ON just below the farmhouse and pass through a gate. A grassy track now leads down hill through a plantation with a variety of young trees. At the bottom of the

WALK 7

UP TO THE BORDER

DESCRIPTION This is a classic circular walk, 5 miles in length. It starts from the atmospheric ruins of Llanthony Abbey and climbs up the steep eastern side of the Honddu valley to gain the Hatterrall ridge and the English border. An easy walk leads north along the ridge, with extensive views across both sides of the border. The return leg descends from the ridge by a well-used path enjoying high-level views of the Priory ruins. This walk can be combined with **Walk 8** to make a fine 9-mile expedition over to the ancient settlement of Longtown on the English side of the ridge. To do this, follow the instructions for this walk as far as point **2**. Then follow **Walk 8** from point **4** into Longtown. Return by following **Walk 8** from the beginning as far as point **3** and then pick up this walk from point **3**. *The walk includes remote moorland and mountain terrain, which require proper clothing and equipment as well as competent use of navigation aids in misty weather.* **Take a compass.**
START Llanthony Priory. SO 289278.
DIRECTIONS Llanthony Priory lies just over 6 miles off the A465 Between Abergavenny and Hereford. Turn off the main road ay Llanfihangel Crucorney and follow the valley road signposted to Llanthony. The starting point can also be reached from Hay on Wye via the minor road over the Gospel Pass. There are toilets and a car park at Llanthony Priory.

See **Walk 3** for background details about Llanthony Priory.

I Leave the car park passing the abbey on your right and the church of St David on your left. Where the access road turns left down the hill, KEEP STRAIGHT AHEAD THROUGH A GATE AND TURN IMMEDIATELY RIGHT up the track signposted to Hatterrall Hill. At the end of the field go through another gate and immediately TURN RIGHT to follow a sign to 'Offa's Dyke South' above the perimeter of the abbey. At the end of the Abbey's wall go through

another gate and BEAR LEFT to climb up the field diagonally. A gate at the top leads in to a wood. Follow the track as it climbs through the trees. At the far end ignore the metal gate ahead. Instead GO THROUGH A WOODEN FIELD GATE TO THE LEFT and climb up the last field with the fence to your right. At the top a final gate leads on to the open hillside. TURN RIGHT and follow the path signposted to Cwmyoy. At first you enjoy some respite as the path follows a level course along a shelf on the hillside, just above the boundary of enclosed land. It weaves through bracken and a scattering of trees before beginning to climb diagonally up the hillside. As you climb, enjoy views down the Vale of Ewyas and on to the Sugar Loaf. Near the upper reaches a wall joins you on the left and the gradient eases. Ignore a branch doubling back to the left and maintain the same direction slanting up the hill. You gain the crest of the ridge at a junction of paths marked with a stone direction post. *This ridge extends for 12 miles from Hatterrall Hill in the south to Hay Bluff, overlooking the Wye valley, in the north. It is the most easterly of the long ridges of the Black Mountains and marks the border between Wales and England for all of its length. It also carries Offa's Dyke Long Distance footpath. This 177-mile odyssey winds its way from Prestatyn to Chepstow, often following the line of the ninth century earthwork erected as a demarcation for Offa's Saxon kingdom. There is no evidence that the Dyke came along this ridge, though fragments have been found further east. However the ridge itself is a definitive border and makes an excellent high-level walk from Pandy to Hay-on-Wye. Ahead the path drops steeply down the other side into Longtown (see **Walk 8**). If you want to visit the summit of Hatterrall Hill, it's a short way to the right.*

2 Our route TURNS LEFT at the junction. A gentle ascent leads to the trig point at 552m. *There are extensive views here and all along the ridge. Down to the east lie the Monnow valley, Cloddock church and the straggling village of Longtown. Beyond are the rolling fields of Herefordshire with distant views to the Cotswolds and Clee Hills on a clear day. To the west, successive ridges of* the Black Mountains march westwards into the hinterlands of Wales. This feels like a border.

3 Half a mile after the trig point a faint path joins from the east. This is the route from Longtown (see **Walk 8**). It matters little if you miss this junction as you carry on north along the ridge for a further ¾ mile, until a stone direction post and a large cairn mark the turning point for Llanthony.

4 TURN LEFT here and follow the clear path. The descent is gentle at first but soon becomes much steeper as the ruins of the priory come into view over the brow of the hill. Although the gradient is serious, the path is clear and easy to negotiate and eventually a stile leads off the open access land. Descend the field beyond it and then cross two more stiles with a small copse between them. More fields lead gently down towards the historic walls of the priory and the starting point.

LONGTOWN & OFFA'S DYKE PATH

DESCRIPTION The old medieval settlement of Longtown lies sheltered beneath the looming heights of the Black Mountains. The village sits on a slight ridge between the River Monnow and the Olchon Brook on the Herefordshire side of the border. This 5-mile circuit of the border is the first of two walks that climb the eastern ridge of the Black Mountains from England. The first part of the ascent lies through fields rising from the Olchon Brook to the base of the Hatterrall ridge. A steep climb then takes you to the top of the ridge, which is the line of the border. An enjoyable walk follows the border south, also accompanying Offa's Dyke long distance path. Descent from the ridge uses an ancient cross-border track between Llanthony and Longtown. **Take a compass.**

START Car park at Longtown Village Hall. SO 324287.

DIRECTIONS Longtown is reached by a minor road, which leaves the A465 at the Pandy Inn, about 6 miles north of Abergavenny. From the north leave the A465 at Pontrilas and travel by another minor road through Ewyas Harold.

*B*efore or after your walk you may like to visit Longtown Castle, which lies a short way up the road from the Village Hall. It was built as an earthen enclosure in 1180 by Walter de Lacy. The impressive stone keep dates from the 13th century and was defended by walls over 4 yards thick. The town never really developed as intended and the castle was abandoned in the fourteenth century. It was briefly reoccupied during Owain Glyndŵr's campaign for Welsh independence in the early 15th century. The castle is now cared for by English Heritage and there is free access at any reasonable time

I From the car park TURN LEFT to follow the road and soon TURN LEFT down a lane. Both 'speed limit ends' and 'no through road' signs mark its start, an interesting combination of rubrics. This lane soon descends to cross the Olchon Brook. Go through the gate on the far side. Soon after passing a static caravan, CROSS A STILE ON THE RIGHT into a field. Pass across the next three fields following a small stream on your right. At the top of the third field CROSS THE WOODEN FOOTBRIDGE and head across the next small field to a gap in the trees. Here BEAR LEFT to ascend the next field diagonally to a gate in the top corner. Don't go through this, instead stay inside the field and follow the fence. Keep ascending to pass through a gap in the next hedge, then reaching a track. FOLLOW THIS TO THE RIGHT, across a ford and on through some farm buildings to reach a road. TURN LEFT and follow the road as it winds up hill.

2 The road bends to the right just after a cattle grid. But at this point, leave the road and TURN LEFT along a green lane. After about 200 yards leave this to BEAR RIGHT up the hillside following a public footpath sign. Follow this well trodden path as it climbs diagonally leftwards above a small, enclosed copse. About 100 yards after you leave the company of this enclosure, the track crosses a sunken path. TURN RIGHT to follow this path as it slants diagonally up to the right. *The Hatterrall Ridge stretches northwards from Pandy past Longtown and towards Hay on Wye. Nowhere perhaps is the border between Wales and England more distinct than here. The fertile rolling hills of Herefordshire face the steep and daunting slopes of this ridge. Indeed some say that the formidable appearance of the hills from the east gave them the title of the Black Mountains. About two-thirds the way up it doubles back to the left and continues its ascent. As it nears the top it veers right, becomes narrower and arrives at a wide path on the crest of the ridge by a small pile of stones. To combine this walk with* **Walk 7** *to Llanthony, turn right here and follow the ridge until you reach point* **3** *on* **Walk 7** *then following the instructions.*

3 Otherwise TURN LEFT to follow the ridge south. It marks both the border

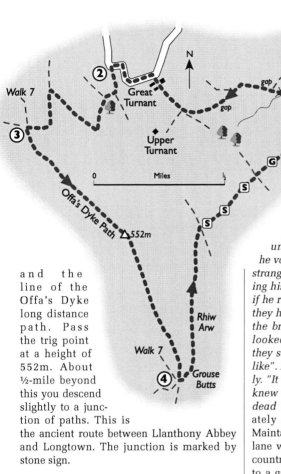

and the line of the Offa's Dyke long distance path. Pass the trig point at a height of 552m. About ½-mile beyond this you descend slightly to a junction of paths. This is the ancient route between Llanthony Abbey and Longtown. The junction is marked by stone sign.

4 TURN LEFT to follow the path towards Longtown. *Although the line of the ridge is clear, travellers have had to exercise care about navigation across it. Ella Mary Leather, a local folk historian, wrote about such a story in 1912. 'A man had been to see friends in Llanthony and was returning over the mountain to Longtown. Then 'a fog' came on suddenly and he lost his way. He was standing, quite at a loss, when a man came towards him, wearing a large broad-brimmed hat and a cloak. He did not speak but beckoned, and the man followed him, until he found himself in the right path. Turning round, he thanked his unknown friend, but received no reply; he vanished quickly in the fog. This seemed strange, but he thought no more till, on visiting his friends at Llanthony later, they asked if he reached home in safety that evening, as they had been anxious. When the stranger in the broad-brimmed hat was described they looked at each other in surprise. "What!" they said, "Tell us exactly what his face was like". He described the stranger more minutely. "It was T— H—, for sure", they cried, "he knew the mountain well, and he has been dead these two years".'* The path immediately descends diagonally down the hill. Maintain this direction until you join a green lane which runs along the edge of the open country. Here the boundary fence dips down to a gateway. CROSS THE STILE next to it, giving access to a passage between two fences. At the bottom of this CROSS ANOTHER STILE and descend the next field to the bottom left corner. Carry on down the left hand side of the next few fields, adjacent to a line of trees and a fence. At the bottom of the last field a gate leads into a farmyard. Go through the farm buildings and on down the concrete access road to cross the Olchon brook. The lane now leads back into Longtown. At the road TURN RIGHT to return to your starting point or turn left to visit the castle.

WALK 9

BLACK HILL

DESCRIPTION A genuine introduction to two common features of the Black Mountains: wild, bleak ridges and well-vegetated isolated valleys. The outward route climbs an airy serrated ridge known colloquially as the 'Cat's Back'. This splendid approach offers wide views across Herefordshire and leads to the summit of Black Hill. A peaty plateau leads to the source of the Olchon Brook, which breaks out of its boggy birthplace through a rocky escarpment known as Darren. The energetic watercourse quickly carves a romantic fertile valley, which is followed back to the starting point, a total of 5 miles.

START Black Hill picnic area and car park. SO 288328.

DIRECTIONS To reach this isolated spot, follow the minor road north from Longtown towards Llanveynoe past the castle. Continue until you pick up signs for the picnic area, directing you to the left.

This is the second of two walks from Herefordshire. However for centuries this part of the county was a disputed area. Local place names are evidence of a distinctly Welsh lilt. The district was known in English as Archenfield and in Welsh as Ergyng depending on your preference. The Domesday Book refers to the disputed nature of the border marches. 'In Archenfield the king has three churches. The priests of these churches undertake the king's embassies into Wales, and each of them sings for the king two masses every week. When any one of them dies, the king customarily has 20s. from him. If any Welshman steals a man or a woman, a horse, an ox, or a cow, on being convicted, he first returns what has been stolen and [then] pays 20s. as a fine. If he kills any thegn's man, he gives 10s. to the lord of the slain man. But if a Welshman kills a Welshman, the relatives of the slain man come together and plunder the slayer and his kin and burn their houses until, toward noon on the following day, the body of the slain man is buried.' The phone box at Llanveynoe carries the title 'Teleffon', showing that even BT is confused.

1 CROSS THE STILE from the car park giving access to the open hillside. Head directly and steeply up the ridge following the grass path between gorse bushes. The ascent is gentler once you have gained the crest. *It is a wonderful walk, giving a sense of freedom. In places the ridge, known locally as the Cat's Back, is less than six feet wide. But the path is broad and easy and views extend west across the Olchon Valley to the ridge marking the contemporary border. Eastwards there is a wide prospect over the Monnow Valley and across Herefordshire to the English Midlands. For much of its life the Monnow forms the border between England and Wales and gives its name to the town and county of Monmouth. However, it starts life as a Herefordshire stream rising firmly on the English side of the mountains. The stone castles that guard its banks at Longtown, Skenfrith and Monmouth illustrate its border credentials.* Soon after passing a wind shelter the ridge widens into a broad shoulder and you ascend gently to the summit of Black Hill, marked by a trig point at 640m.

2 From the trig point, BEAR LEFT and keep following the distinct path across rather boggy level moorland terrain. Follow the path for just under a mile. A small pile of stones on the path marks the junction with a bridleway. It could be easy to miss so watch out.

3 TURN SHARP LEFT to follow this route. It's a bridleway, though it's actually quite a narrow path. It soon begins to descend to a depression. Soon after a ruined shelter the depression is suddenly transformed into a steep sided valley and the stream descends a deep ravine. The Olchon Valley opens out in front of you and the path descends to the left of the stream. *It is rocky at first but then becomes a delightful grassy track among carpets of bilberry.*

4 Below a wood a gate gives access to a sunken lane, which can be rather muddy. But soon it joins a tarmac lane. Follow this in the same direction for about 1¼ miles. *It is extremely quiet, just serving farms at the head of the valley and the hedgerows*

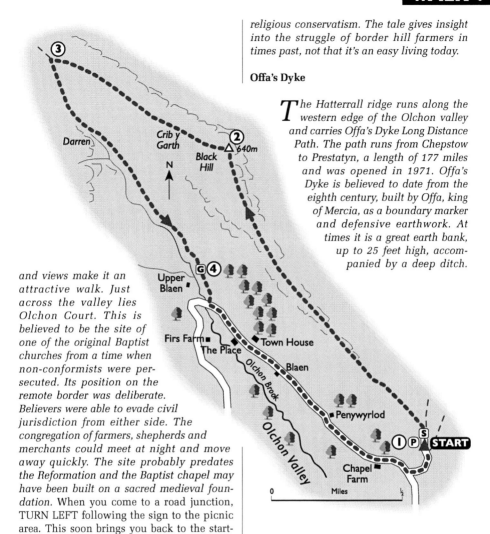

religious conservatism. The tale gives insight into the struggle of border hill farmers in times past, not that it's an easy living today.

Offa's Dyke

*T*he Hatterrall ridge runs along the western edge of the Olchon valley and carries Offa's Dyke Long Distance Path. The path runs from Chepstow to Prestatyn, a length of 177 miles and was opened in 1971. Offa's Dyke is believed to date from the eighth century, built by Offa, king of Mercia, as a boundary marker and defensive earthwork. At times it is a great earth bank, up to 25 feet high, accompanied by a deep ditch.

and views make it an attractive walk. Just across the valley lies Olchon Court. This is believed to be the site of one of the original Baptist churches from a time when non-conformists were persecuted. Its position on the remote border was deliberate. Believers were able to evade civil jurisdiction from either side. The congregation of farmers, shepherds and merchants could meet at night and move away quickly. The site probably predates the Reformation and the Baptist chapel may have been built on a sacred medieval foundation. When you come to a road junction, TURN LEFT following the sign to the picnic area. This soon brings you back to the starting point.

'On the Black Hill'

*B*lack Hill was the setting for the novel by Bruce Chatwin, 'On the Black Hill', which was made into a film in 1987. The moving story tells of twins who grow up together and spend all their lives in the hard graft of agricultural work on the land. For 80 years their lives are stifled by hardship, pride and

In other places more modest features remain. There is little of the earthwork to be seen between Monmouth and Knighton, with just a few possible remains around Hereford. The route of the Dyke is a matter of speculation here. There is no evidence that it followed the Hatterrall ridge, but it makes a splendid route for the footpath. Parts of it are included in **Walks 4**, **7** and **8** but the whole 17-mile section from Pandy to Hay can be walked in a day. (Take equipment for a long mountain walk, including a compass.)

TRETOWER, CEFN MOEL AND CWM CLARACH

DESCRIPTION A 7-mile tour of valley and mountain countryside, enjoying a wide variety of scenery and terrain. Starting from historic Tretower, the route crosses the Rhiangoll's flood plain to reach the site of a Roman fort. A climb up to the Cefn Moel ridge yields views over Llangorse Lake and the Brecon Beacons. The descent through a charming wooded valley brings you back to the river at Cwmdu, from where an old green road completes the circuit to Tretower.

START Tretower Court and Castle. SO 186213.

DIRECTIONS The village of Tretower is on the A479 between Crickhowell and Talgarth, a mile from its junction with the A40 at Nant-y-ffin. A lane leads from the A479 to Tretower Court. There is space to park at the roadside opposite the entrance.

Tretower has always been at an important crossroads close to the confluence of the Usk and Rhiangoll. So perhaps it is unsurprising that there are two historic buildings on the same site here. The thirteenth century stone keep superseded an early Norman castle. Next to it is a rare example of a late medieval manor house. The present building dates from the fifteenth century. Both are in the care of Cadw and are open to the public (admission charge).

I WALK ALONG THE LANE by the church of St John the Evangelist. You pass the round tower and walls of Tretower castle on your left. *Some of the walls have been built into barns.* At the end of the village you pass another old chapel, now a house, on your right. Straight ahead is a gate with a public footpath sign to Gaer. GO THROUGH THE GATE and cross the field. At the far end a concrete bridge crosses the Rhiangoll and a

gate admits you to the next field. Keep to its right hand side next to a hedge. At the end pass through a gap and continue along the left hand edge of the next two fields, with a stile in the corner between them. At the end of the second field another stile access to a lane. TURN LEFT and follow the lane between two fences. Keep straight on past a group of houses including Lower Gaer Farm, where the lane becomes metalled. At the end of the lane come a T-junction and TURN RIGHT. Follow the lane as it weaves round and then climbs up Pen-y-gaer. *This is the site of a small Roman fort built half way along the Roman road from Brecon to Abergavenny.* Descend to another T-junction.

2 Immediately OPPOSITE THE JUNCTION CROSS A STILE that leads to an old lane almost overwhelmed by trees and undergrowth. To follow the right of way, climb two fields adjacent to this overgrown lane. At the top the second field, continue to follow its edge as it curves to the left. WATCH FOR A STILE in the hedge on the upper boundary. CROSS THIS AND CONTINUE UP the left hand edge of this final field. At the top a gate leads to a lane.

3 TURN RIGHT, pass a house and GO THROUGH A GATE THEN TURNING IMMEDIATELY LEFT up a green lane. Climb up this bridleway between trees and hedges alongside a small stream. At the top a gate leads to open land and a metalled road. CONTINUE STRAIGHT ACROSS THE ROAD and carry on up the wide track as it climbs through bracken and gorse, avoiding any deviations. After a while it levels out meets a wall on the crest of the ridge. KEEP THE WALL ON YOUR LEFT AND FOLLOW THE TRACK. *Soon you enjoy views left over Llangorse Lake.* Ignore any side turnings and keep on the main track. The wall gives way to a fence as you start a further gentle ascent, *topped by a small scar. 200 yards along the scar is the site of a prehistoric burial mound.* Soon after this there a slight descent leads to a major junction of paths marked by a small cairn right in the middle of the track and a group of larch trees 100 yards to your left.

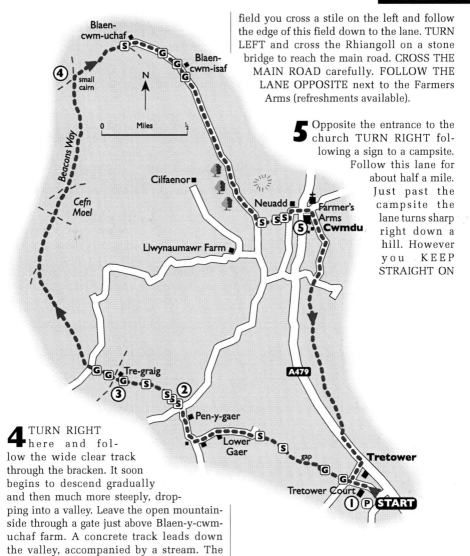

field you cross a stile on the left and follow the edge of this field down to the lane. TURN LEFT and cross the Rhiangoll on a stone bridge to reach the main road. CROSS THE MAIN ROAD carefully. FOLLOW THE LANE OPPOSITE next to the Farmers Arms (refreshments available).

5 Opposite the entrance to the church TURN RIGHT following a sign to a campsite. Follow this lane for about half a mile. Just past the campsite the lane turns sharp right down a hill. However you KEEP STRAIGHT ON

4 TURN RIGHT here and follow the wide clear track through the bracken. It soon begins to descend gradually and then much more steeply, dropping into a valley. Leave the open mountainside through a gate just above Blaen-y-cwm-uchaf farm. A concrete track leads down the valley, accompanied by a stream. The lane passes through another farmyard and then continues, more level, along a charming valley with hedgerows of wild flowers and fields decorated with ash trees. After a while the lane descends again through thicker woodland. At the bottom of the hill CROSS A STILE ON THE LEFT marked with a Beacons Way sign. Follow the left hand side of the field as it crosses the bottom of the valley. *The village and church tower of Cwm Du lie ahead.* Just before the end of the

here past the farm signs onto a green lane, an avenue between trees. *From this raised terrace on the side of the hill there are good views across the valley.* It continues for about a mile before joining the main road. TURN LEFT to walk along it. There is no alternative to 300 yards along the edge of this busy road. Take care, as there is no footpath. Just after the first house in the village TURN RIGHT down a very narrow lane. At the end of the lane TURN LEFT to return to Tretower Court.

WALK 11

Y DERI &
THE SUGAR
LOAF

DESCRIPTION A 5½-mile circular route that climbs one of the and most famous and distinctive of the Black Mountains. A gentle ascent through oak woodlands gives way to a splendid gorse covered ridge. The approach to the summit makes use of a spiral pathway that gives excellent all round views. Outstanding views and a sense of open space maintain interest throughout this classic conquest of one of the best-known Black Mountains.

START Llwyn Du car park GR SO 288167.

DIRECTIONS There is a small car park at Llwyn Du on the southern slopes of the Sugar Loaf. From Abergavenny town centre, follow the A40 towards Brecon for about ½ mile. Turn right, shortly before Neville Hall Hospital, to take Chapel Road. This rises northwards through residential areas and becomes a narrow lane as it leaves the town. It ends at a small car park at Llwyn Du. *Take a compass.*

1 Take the roughly surfaced lane continuing north from the car park. After a short way cross an old cattle grid and pass the National Trust sign to enter Parc Lodge. Continue on the track as it gently descends to cross the Afon Cibi. Shortly after, turn sharp RIGHT onto another forest track, now heading south on the opposite slope of the valley. Enjoy the oak woodlands, rich in birdsong, with the Afon Cibi gurgling down to your right.

2 By two cottages TURN SHARP LEFT and enter the National Trust's Y Deri land through a gate. *Almost all the Sugar Loaf is in the care of the National Trust, giving open access across wide and open countryside. On the south side, grassy spurs topped with springy turf, bracken and gorse, rise out of delightfully wooded valleys, giving a variety of excellent approaches to the mountain. This route uses one of these sylvan ascents to* gain Y Deri ridge, following this to the summit. Climb steadily up a good track through the woods. Maintain this direction as the woods give way to more open bracken and gorse heath on the upper slopes. Pass a wall corner and soon reach the top of the ridge with prospects eastwards over the Skirrid (see **Walk 20**).

3 A good track leads northwards along the ridge. *The well-drained, springy turf makes for easy and pleasant walking and there are excellent views all around, with the Sugar Loaf now rising up to the left.* After just over a mile, you reach a gate with a track leading back into the Parc Lodge enclosure. Ignore this and keep outside the fence, following a path along its perimeter until you reach a junction with a small path to the RIGHT, leading directly towards the summit. There is a small holly tree on the left to confirm your navigation.

4 This track rises gently, and then more steeply as it approaches the summit. It is possible to make a beeline for the highest point, but it is far better to stick to the grassy path as it circumnavigates the upper cone of the mountain, like a turfed spiral staircase. *This is not only a gentler ascent, but also gives ever-changing views right round the mountain. First northwards over the Grwyne Fawr valley, then towards the bleak highest ground of the Black Mountains around Waun Fach, then westwards up the Usk valley and finally south across Llanwenarth Common and Abergavenny to the Blorenge. Shattered rocks mark the summit and the concise, shapely plateau is crowned by a trig point marking its height of 596m. The distinctive conical summit of the Sugar Loaf is a landmark for many miles around. Its profile can be made out from the Cotswold escarpment 50 miles to the east. The peak, known in Welsh as Pen y Fal, marks the gateway to the upper Usk valley, drawing the eye west into the hills and mountains of the interior of Wales.*

5 From the top a path slants downwards across the southern face of the summit. This becomes stony, but ignore the steps and grassier path which turns down to the right and maintain the course you started. The gradient becomes kinder and the terrain is less rocky as you drop down through the heather.

6 At a junction of paths VEER LEFT to reach a gate just 100 yards away. Cross the stile to re-enter the Parc Lodge estate. The public footpath passes down the middle of a field, through a series of gates by a small wood and continues to descend, becoming a wider track. The way continues down through a succession of fields, dotted with mature trees and leads you back to the car park at Llwyn Du.

Sugar Loaf

CWM GWENFFRWD & THE SUGAR LOAF

DESCRIPTION This 5½–mile walk approaches the Sugar Loaf from the west. You can climb directly from Llangenny but parking is not easy there. So this route starts from the excellent car park on Llanwenarth Common. Instead of the well-trodden direct ascent, the walk makes use of a good network of tracks around the wooded shoulder of the mountain. After crossing Cwm Gwenffrwd, a pleasant ridge path leads onto the spur of Mynydd Pen-y-fal before striking out directly for the summit of the mountain.
START Car Park on Llanwenarth Common. SO 267167.
DIRECTIONS A narrow lane leaves the A40 on the western outskirts of Abergavenny. Signs to Sugar Loaf Vineyard point you in the right direction. Pass the vineyard to continue climbing up the slopes of the Sugar Loaf. After a while the lane turns west and climbs around the side of the mountain to reach a good car park. This is an excellent viewpoint over the Usk valley and the Brecon Beacons. It also offers a bird's eye view of Abergavenny. Identification of features is aided by a toposcope. *Take a compass.*

I From the car park continue along the tarmac lane westwards. *Enjoy extensive views across the Usk valley to Gilwern and the Clydach Gorge. This narrow valley carries the main road up to the 'heads of the valleys' en route to Merthyr and Swansea. Two hundred years ago it was a hive of industrial activity and a centre for iron making. Today old tramways and abandoned limestone quarries invite careful exploration, and this environment has proved a fertile ground for plants in the nature reserve situated here.* The lane bends past Llyweddrog Farm and continues to meander through a series of fields studded with a variety of trees. After a while you pass a series of farm buildings at Pen-y-graig.

2 Just beyond these you come to a T-junction and TURN RIGHT. Holly and hazel bushes form an avenue for the lane as it passes across fields and then descends through a wood. Go straight across a junction of tracks and continue past the house at Cwm-cegyr. Curve round to cross the stream. Pass through a gate. *This is Cwm Gwenffrwd, a charming wooded valley. The echo of birdsong mingles with the gentle babbling of the brook as it carries water from the Sugar Loaf down to the Grwyne and the Usk.*

3 About 200 yards beyond the gate TURN SHARP RIGHT up a track signposted to 'The Hill'. The path emerges from the woods to curve to the right, ascending a field with a fence on the left, now heading straight for the Sugar Loaf. *A lovely variety of trees graces the far bank of the stream.* At the top of the field cross a stile next to a gate and continue on the bridleway. Soon a gate gives access to the open hillside.

4 Just before you cross the stream TURN SHARP LEFT to ascend a grassy track slanting up through the bracken. *As it levels out it curves round to the right opening up the prospect of the highest tops of the Black Mountains, the Usk valley and the Brecon Beacons.* On the brow of the hill, opposite a gate giving access to a bridleway, TURN RIGHT to follow a path climbing the crest of the ridge. As you gain the top of the ridge you join another path coming up from the left and CURVE RIGHT for a direct assault on the summit. A straightforward grassy track leads inexorably to the shattered rocks of the summit cone. The highest point is marked with a trig point at 596m. *The view from here takes in the Black Mountains to the north, the Brecon Beacons to the west and the edge of the South Wales iron and coal belt to the south. The strategic position of Abergavenny is evident to the south-east, guarding the entrance to the upper Usk valley and the route through to West Wales. Here was the Roman fort of Gobannium. The remains of a Norman castle offers evidence of its importance in later centuries. During the industrial revolution it was a garrison town, with soldiers used to subdue the vola-*

tility of the nearby industrial towns, when the need arose.

5 To return from the summit DESCEND BY THE TRACK that heads west-south-west (*240 degrees*) from the summit. In mist you will need a compass to confirm your direction, though the path is unmistakeable once you've found it. After a stony start it soon becomes a wide grassy passageway that descends gracefully down the mountain, gradually curving around the head of Cwm Trosnant. *The lower south-facing slopes of the mountain offer protection from the harshest weather. Vines have been grown here and* in other nearby spots in recent years. At a crossing of paths above the cwm you TURN RIGHT to follow another grassy track curving gently down to the car park.

ALTERNATIVE DIRECT ASCENT

If you're short of time, the direct descent could be used for the outward climb as well. It makes a straightforward and easy walk, mostly on well-drained, grassy tracks. But, remember, the Sugar Loaf's summit is over 2,000 feet above sea level and you should be prepared for unexpected weather.

CWMYOY

DESCRIPTION Cwmyoy invites exploration. Seen from the valley road between Llanfihangel and Llanthony, the village appears to perch below a landslip on the far side of the River Honddu. This short but interesting walk is ideal for a stroll on a summer evening or when time is limited. Crossing the River Honddu and its adjacent meadows, the route passes through Cwmyoy village with its crooked church before venturing into the picturesque Cwm Iau. The walk returns to the village by climbing around the back of the landslip, though the going is straightforward enough. The total distance is 2½ miles.

START Cwmyoy Village Hall. SO 301226.

DIRECTIONS Cwmyoy Village Hall is on the road between Llanfihangel Crucorney and Llanthony, on the other side of the river from Cwmyoy village itself. There are some car parking spaces outside the village hall unless it's being used. It is practically impossible to park anywhere in Cwmyoy village, though there are two or three spaces just above the church.

1 A stile leads from the road by the house next to the car park. CROSS THIS and go down the small field, pass through a gate and veer left across the second field to reach a wooden footbridge. Cross the Honddu on this bridge and follow the footpath through the field with the fence on your left. On reaching the lane TURN LEFT and follow it until a junction near a red telephone box.

2 TURN RIGHT and follow this lane through the village as it winds up hill, passing the entrance to the church on your left. Just beyond this entrance reach another junction and TURN RIGHT with a sign to Penywern ('No Through Road'). Pass Penywern farmhouse on your left and go straight through the gate ahead, which gives access to wide track. Follow this through a series of fields, passing a cottage, until you reach a group of derelict buildings known as Ty-hwnt-y-bwlch, including a mustard-

coloured mansion house. *Cwm Iau is an appealing place. The patchwork of fields gives way to the bracken-clad slopes of the mountains. Opposite, the ridge of Hatterrall Hill reaches out of the valley, carrying the English border and the Offa's Dyke footpath on their journey northwards into Mid Wales.*

3 At the far end of the buildings and next to a ruined barn, follow the track SHARP LEFT. It now passes above the buildings. Cross a stile and continue on the track. Just beyond some old metal sheds and before a house TURN RIGHT up a steep path, between a wall and a fence. On your left are the shattered rocky buttresses of Cwmyoy landslip. *The top of the landslip is now open access land and can be reached from here. It offers a bird's eye view of the village and the Vale of Ewyas.* As you reach the saddle there is a stile in the fence on your right. CROSS THIS and follow the grassy path down the hill until you reach a gate.

4 Do not go through the gate. Instead TURN LEFT and follow the narrow path by the left hand side of the fence. Soon you pass through a gate and the path becomes a lane between two fences. This drops down below some woods, soon passing a wooden chalet. Where the lane veers left and starts climbing, TURN RIGHT through a green gate and follow a rather gloomy sunken lane, which emerges in Cwmyoy just above the church. TURN LEFT to pass above the church. *From here you can appreciate the contorted nature of the building with a curving roof on the nave and a distinctly crooked tower. The church is dedicated to St Martin of Tours, a fourth century soldier from Tours in modern day France. He was known as a theologian but also for his generosity. He once cut his own cloak in half, giving part to a beggar. The church dates from the Middle Ages.* At the end of this lane TURN RIGHT to rejoin the outward route. Follow the lane as it curves down through the village, TURNING LEFT by the red phone box. Down the lane, cross a stile on the RIGHT to pass through fields back to the village hall.

St Martin's Church, Cwmyoy

*T*he village of Cwmyoy derives its name from the Welsh words for valley of the yoke. It refers to the side valley, a deep recess into the Hatterrall ridge, overlooked by this walk. Its shape apparently resembles the yoke of an ox. The church is chronically irregular. There are few right angles from any perspective, due to the underlying rock. Its tower leans at a greater angle than its distant cousin in Pisa. It occupies a picturesque site on the side of the valley. The tower contains six bells which date from 1672, and the eighteenth century communion table is still in use. It is normally open during daylight hours.

St Martin's Church

AROUND TWYN-Y-GAER

DESCRIPTION This is an enjoyable 5-mile saunter with much of historical interest. From the car park a steady ascent leads to a wooded promenade along the southern side of the Vale of Ewyas. An Iron Age fort caps the summit of Twyn-y-Gaer with panoramic views over three valleys. A shady lane leads down from the common with westward views across the Grwyne Fawr valley while the return route follows a high level green road, commanding views of Cwm Coed-y-Cerrig and the Sugar Loaf.

START Walkers' Car Park just north of the Queen's Head Inn. SO 311222.

DIRECTIONS The Queen's Head Inn is situated 1½ miles along the Llanthony road from its junction with the A465 at Llanfihangel Crucorney. The Walkers' Car Park is on the opposite side of the road. A daily £1 charge is requested and should be paid at the pub.

1 Ascend the steep tarmac lane, which leaves the valley road at the entrance to the car park. A steady climb leads through the woods up the ridge of Twyn-y-Gaer. Eventually the tarmac ends and the ascent gives way to a level promenade. *This is a charming, easy walk and through the trees you can survey the Vale of Ewyas below. The prospect includes the crooked church and landslip at Cwmyoy on the other side of the valley (see **Walk 13**). A little further along the steep cliffs of Darren rise abruptly to the high moorland and the English border.*

2 Pass through a gate to enter the open land. Immediately TURN LEFT and climb up a broad grassy track through the bracken. It veers to the left just below the highest part of the hill and then attacks the summit from the east. A cairn marks the top at 427m. *The summit plateau is a delightful grassy promenade, studded with gorse bushes. It's easy to see why the ancient Britons chose this site, perched on a hilltop overlooking three valleys. The ditches and ramparts*

*are still discernable. The fort is oval in shape and covers an area of over 4 acres. It consists of three sections, surrounded by a double embankment. From the top you can see the sites of two neighbouring forts. Eastwards lies Trewyn at the southern end of the Hatterrall ridge, while Crug Hywel crowns the Table Mountain above Crickhowell (see **Walks 16 & 17**).* At the top carry STRAIGHT ON past the cairn to the end of the summit plateau. A deep defensive ditch marks the boundary of the fort. It is easiest to cross this at the left hand end, then picking up a clear grassy path SLOPING DOWNHILL TO THE RIGHT. After a short steep section, there's a graceful descent through the bracken to the wide saddle of the ridge. *From here you can see the ridge ahead is quite narrow and the valleys either side are not far apart. But they drain in completely different directions. To the left, the Grwyne Fawr's waters supply the Usk, eventually passing under Newport's transporter bridge to join the Bristol Channel. To the left the Honddu unites with the Monnow a few miles north, and the water then flows to the Wye and on to the Severn at Chepstow.*

3 At the bottom you come to a wall and meet a track running alongside it. BEAR LEFT to join this track and continue along it. In about 500 yards you pass a house set back on the right. About 300 yards further you reach a junction of tracks.

4 TURN SHARP LEFT here, doubling back to a southerly direction. Follow this lane just above a wall and a wood and just below the crest of the ridge.

5 Close to a ruined hut another track leads downhill sharply to the right. *To join up with **Walk 6** to Patrishow and the Grwyne Valley, turn right and follow this bridleway downhill for 500 yards, reaching the farmhouse at Ty Mawr.* To stay on this walk, ignore the turning and carry STRAIGHT ON keeping to the green lane, which is now enclosed. A gate leads to a walled lane, which descends gently with views across the Grwyne Fawr and over to the Sugar Loaf. Towards the bottom, the lane is joined by a concrete track from the left and becomes roughly surfaced as it approaches some farm buildings. Follow the road past New Inn Farm and the whitewashed cottages.

6 Just below the farm and next to a telegraph pole, TURN SHARP LEFT to follow a lane, which may be muddy here, and pass through a gate. Avoid side turnings to a quarry and ascend steadily on the track through oak, holly and hazel trees. *As the lane levels out enjoy south facing views over Cwm Coed-y-Cerrig and the National Nature Reserve, managed by the Countryside Council for Wales. The boggy area in the bottom of the valley includes many alder trees and offers a good habitat for frogs. Higher up the hillside, towards the course of our walk, drier terrain supports mixed woodland including oak, ash, beech and hazel. The secretive Dormouse can be found here, so look out! If you want to visit*

the reserve itself, the car park can be reached by way of the road towards Forest Coalpit. On the highest section of the route a cinder track provides a sensible a diversion around a house. A gate leads to a walled lane, which descends through the trees and joins your outward route. TURN RIGHT to walk down the lane to the car park.

Twyn-y-gaer

*T*he local Silures tribe fought the Romans from the hill fort at Twyn-y-Gaer. More evidence of a turbulent past is found a little further along the ridge to the north of this walk. The Revenge Stone, Y Ddial Garreg, commemorates the spot where local Welsh tenants struck back at a tyrannical Norman overlord (SO 284243).

MYNYDD LLYSIAU & THE GRWYNE FECHAN

DESCRIPTION This is a delightful 9½-mile excursion into one of the remotest recesses of the Black Mountains. The outward leg climbs from the foot of Cwm Banw. Once the modest climb to Tal Trwymau is complete you have the prospect of a gentle ridge walk with superb views all the way to the isolated mountain pass at the head of the Grwyne Fechan valley. From here the return route makes use of a clear and well-graded path known as Macnamara's road. It skirts the wild hillside before crossing the river at Tal-y-maes Bridge. The lower reaches are adorned by woodland before a final lane walk offers lush hedgerows decked in wild flowers.

START A small parking area just next to a bridge at Cwm Banw, in the Grwyne Fechan valley. SO 234229

DIRECTIONS From Crickhowell, a minor road leads north from the A40 and into the Grwyne Fechan valley. Just after a sharp bend and a bridge, there is a small parking area by the road. There is enough space for about five cars.

I Cross the stile next to the parking area and BEAR RIGHT to follow a permissive path up hill using marker posts as a guide. At the top of the field go through a gateway and TURN LEFT up an enclosed track following a sign, 'To the Mountain'. After a while go through another gate and keep to the main track ascending up the ridge with a wall on your left. *Views now open up ahead to the top of the Grwyne Fechan valley and beyond. Small conifer plantations and bracken add colour to the hillside. To the left the view lies across Cwm Banw to the limestone massif of Pen Cerrig-calch.* Climb past a plantation then cross a stile. Keep to the main track as it ascends to a substantial cairn on the crest of the ridge. From here a broad grassy path ascends gently along the broad ridge past some old quarry workings. A pleasant, easy walk follows a distinct route and offers excellent views with the bulk of Pen Allt-mawr now dominating the western outlook. The ridge swells to the summit of Pen Twyn Glas. *Now views north encompass the Rhiangoll valley and Mynydd Troed. To the south-west, the distinctive profile of the Brecon Beacons presides over the horizon.*

2 At Pen Twyn Glas KEEP STRAIGHT AHEAD along a narrow but clear path across a rather soggy saddle. Soon a boundary stone crowns the top of a small knoll. Continue past this following the broad path slightly left leading towards the top of Mynydd Llysiau. You could be forgiven for missing the summit, a negligible swelling marked only by a few stones. But this is a minor defect in a mountain with such a grand prospect. *The view north is magnificent. The proud form of Mynydd Troed does bear resemblance to the outline of a foot, as its Welsh name implies. You can see the ancient site of Castell Dinas guarding the head of the Rhiangoll valley (see **Walk 5**) and beyond the Wye Valley towards Builth and Hay. A short but steep descent now leads to a high mountain pass. This is an important junction of six mountain paths, at an isolated spot 618m above sea level. To the sharp left a well-engineered route leads into Cwm Nant-yr-ychen. Another route bears left and soon splits into two. Both these lead to the upper reaches of the Rhiangoll valley. One takes the contoured descent along Rhiw Trumau followed on Walks 5 and 17. The path straight ahead climbs the steep ridge to Pen Trumau and on to Waun Fach, the highest peak in the Black Mountains. This major junction and neat pass is unnamed on maps but it deserves a title. Bwlch Trumau might be a suitable description. In front of you lies the very head of the Grwyne Fechan, spawned by drainage down the extensive flank of Waun Fach. A myriad of boggy springs combine to give birth to the infant river whose waters have driven a deep trench southwards through the hills.*

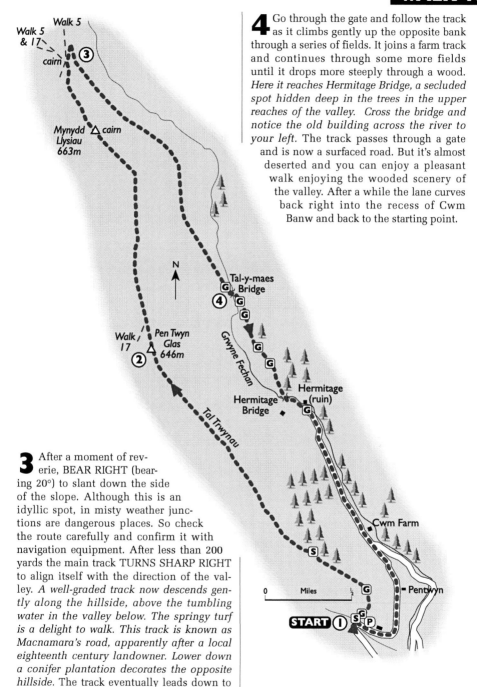

4 Go through the gate and follow the track as it climbs gently up the opposite bank through a series of fields. It joins a farm track and continues through some more fields until it drops more steeply through a wood. *Here it reaches Hermitage Bridge, a secluded spot hidden deep in the trees in the upper reaches of the valley. Cross the bridge and notice the old building across the river to your left.* The track passes through a gate and is now a surfaced road. But it's almost deserted and you can enjoy a pleasant walk enjoying the wooded scenery of the valley. After a while the lane curves back right into the recess of Cwm Banw and back to the starting point.

3 After a moment of reverie, BEAR RIGHT (bearing 20°) to slant down the side of the slope. Although this is an idyllic spot, in misty weather junctions are dangerous places. So check the route carefully and confirm it with navigation equipment. After less than 200 yards the main track TURNS SHARP RIGHT to align itself with the direction of the valley. *A well-graded track now descends gently along the hillside, above the tumbling water in the valley below. The springy turf is a delight to walk. This track is known as Macnamara's road, apparently after a local eighteenth century landowner. Lower down a conifer plantation decorates the opposite hillside.* The track eventually leads down to the river and crosses it at Tal-y-maes Bridge.

WALK 16
TABLE MOUNTAIN & PEN CERRIG-CALCH

DESCRIPTION This 6-mile walk climbs from the centre of Crickhowell to the flat-topped summit of Table Mountain, crowned with an Iron Age fort. It rises north of the town, which derives its name from the fort's Welsh title of Crug Hywel. Beyond Table Mountain a climb leads to the limestone dome of Pen Cerrig-calch, at 701m the highest point of the walk.

START The main car park in Crickhowell. SO 218184.

DIRECTIONS Crickhowell lies on the A40, about 7 miles from Abergavenny and 13 miles from Brecon. The pay-and-display car park is signposted from the A40 in the town centre.

I Walk through the town following the main road towards Brecon. Just after a petrol station, TURN RIGHT up Llanbedr Road. At the end of the houses it becomes a narrow lane. At the junction with Great Oak Road KEEP LEFT with Table Mountain rising straight ahead. Opposite an electricity sub station, TURN LEFT through a gate and follow a walled lane, a public footpath. At the top of the lane cross the stile into the farmyard and TURN RIGHT in front of the house. Pass though a gate and walk across the field with the hedge on your left. At the end of the field another gate leads to a footpath enclosed between two hedges. TURN LEFT and follow the path. At the top a stile leads into a field. Climb up the right hand side of the next two fields. Then a stile leads on to a farm track. TURN LEFT and follow the track as it turns up hill through a gateway and stile into a field. The track ends here but the path continues up the right hand side of this field

next to the hedge. At the top of the field, cross a stile and TURN RIGHT, following the footpath as it climbs up through the woods above a house. At the top of the wood, a stile gives access to the open hillside. The summit of the Table Mountain lies up to the left and a path leads steeply through the bracken to gain the rocky plateau.

2 From the top, descend the northern flank across the remains of the defensive ditch and gain the saddle of land just below the rocky summit. Follow the broad path across the saddle and on up the slopes of the Pen Cerrig-calch. At the top of the steep section a steady but gentler ascent heads towards a cairn on the skyline. From the cairn a short walk through shattered rocks leads to the trig point and a nearby wind shelter.

3 From here retrace steps to the saddle below the summit of the Table Mountain, unless you want to carry on along the ridge on **Walk 17**.

4 At the saddle, TURN RIGHT to follow a path through the bracken, which weaves a route just above the boundary of enclosed land below. Eventually it descends more steeply to some ruins then a small copse of mature trees.

5 It leaves open country through a couple of sheepfolds before going through a gate into a walled lane which leads to a lovely field surrounded by a variety of trees. The route follows the left hand side of the field, crossing a small stream to a gate in the corner. This leads to a lane descending through woodland. At the point where the lane bends left through a gate, leave it in favour of a stile marked with a footpath sign. Follow this path down through fields to the houses of Crickhowell. At the bottom a sign guides you through the houses, past a school, to the A40. Follow this left to return to the start.

1 Follow directions for **Walk 16** until point **3**, the summit of Pen Cerrig-calch.

3 Instead of returning from the summit of Pen Cerrig-calch, CONTINUE ALONG THE PATH THAT HEADS NORTH-WEST along the ridge. After ½ mile it veers north and a gentle ascent leads to the summit of Pen Allt-mawr at 719m. The path then descends more steeply from the summit to pass around the head of Cwm Banw and on to Pen Twyn Glas.

4 At Pen Twyn Glas KEEP STRAIGHT AHEAD along a narrow but clear path across a rather soggy saddle. Soon a boundary stone crowns the top of a small knoll. Continue past this following the broad path slightly left leading towards the top of Mynydd Llysiau. A short but steep descent now leads to a high mountain pass, marked by a cairn and the junction of six mountain routes.

5 From here follow the instructions in **Walk 5** (from point **6**). This brings you to the Castle Inn at Pengenffordd, at the highest point on the Crickhowell to Talgarth road. *Like many linear walks the main problem is the return. Public transport between Pengenffordd and Crickhowell is limited to a weekly bus to Abergavenny market (Tuesday). If you walk the extra 3 miles from Pengenffordd into Talgarth (there is a quiet lane) you can return to Crickhowell by bus via Brecon.*

WALK 17
ALONG THE ROOF OF THE MOUNTAINS

DESCRIPTION This 10-mile linear traverse of the western side of the Black Mountains offers spectacular views and a sense of space and freedom. The walk continues from Pen Cerrig-calch to follow a high level ridge walk taking in four peaks before dropping to the important pass at Pengenffordd, close to Wales' highest castle.

START As **Walk 16**, the main car park in Crickhowell. SO 218184.

DIRECTIONS See **Walk 16**.

WALK 18

LLANFOIST & HILL'S TRAMROAD

DESCRIPTION A fascinating 7-mile exploration around the Blorenge, the 'iron mountain'. The route follows the course of an early nineteenth century tramway system designed to bring pig iron from Blaenavon down to the canal at Llanfoist. A steep climb from the canal starts the walk. Once up the slopes of the incline, you follow a well-graded path around the mountain and through the Punchbowl nature reserve. A quiet lane leads to the summit of the walk at the Keeper's Pond. The return route follows the line of Hill's Tramroad around the side of the Blorenge with spectacular views up the Usk Valley.

START Llanfoist Crossing car park. SO 286134.

DIRECTIONS Llanfoist village lies on the B4246 just a mile south of Abergavenny on the way to Govilon and Blaenavon. To reach Llanfoist you can leave the A465 'Heads of the Valleys' road at an access point a mile east of its junction with the A40, close to a supermarket. The car park also serves the cycle way, built on the course of an old railway.

I From the car park entrance cross the road and head up the lane to the right of the church, signposted 'The Blorenge'. Where the lane ends continue on the footpath through a tunnel under the canal. *The far side brings you to Llanfoist Wharf, the bottom of a series of inclines that brought iron from Blaenavon. A couple of replica trams remind you of its history. The incline was worked by gravity. Loaded trams going downhill pulled the empty ones back up the slope.* Continue straight up the path through the woods, an unremittingly steep climb through woods beside a stream. *Many of the stone sleepers that held the two-feet gauge track in place can still be seen. The top of the first part of the incline is marked by an old brick building, which houses a cistern*

for a nearby farm. Keep straight ahead and climb on up the hill, crossing some side-tracks and a number of stiles. Eventually come to the boundary of open land. Cross a stile and immediately cross another one adjacent to the fell gate.

2 TURN LEFT, ignoring the sign to Garnddyrys, and follow the level path just above the intake wall. Enjoy the views of Abergavenny as you round the side of the hill. After a while a gate gives access to a Woodland Trust nature reserve. Continue through the reserve on a good path. *The faint buzz of noise from the valley is drowned by birdsong. Green woodpeckers, buzzards and tawny owls can be seen here and a variety of woodland birds fly from the range of trees scattered across the hillside. The path comes to a small lake in a glacial hollow known as the Punchbowl.* Cross the retaining bank and follow the path up a hill beside a wall. A gate leads to a sunken lane. Follow the edge of this as it levels out and comes to another gate.

3 Go through the gate and TURN RIGHT onto the lane. The lane climbs gently for about a mile, a pleasant and easy walk across the high moors. The summit is reached at two masts by the Foxhunter car park. Continue beyond this and the road descends a further half-mile to a T-junction. TURN RIGHT to arrive at Pen-ffordd-goch Pond, universally known as the Keeper's Pond. *It was one of a series of reservoirs that fed the forges lower down the mountain.*

4 Follow the cinder path on the edge of the pond. At the end, cross a wooden footbridge and turn left down a grassy path to the main road. TURN LEFT for a few yards before TURNING RIGHT off the road, following the footpath sign to Garnddyrys. Just over 100 yards along here bear RIGHT at a sign to Cwm Llanwenarth. Descend on the narrow grassy path with bracken on one side and heather on the other as it drops down the side of Cwm Siencyn. *This is an old community footpath know as the Rhiw Ifor. A signpost marks its junction with a level track contouring round the mountain.*

This is the course of Hill's Tramroad. Built in the 1820s by Thomas Hill this remarkable feat of engineering carried iron and coal from Blaenavon. At the beginning of the nineteenth century expensive tolls and rough terrain made the land journey down the Eastern Valley dif-

Blorenge

△ 559m

Garnddyrys

Punchbowl

Cwm Craf

Wharf

START ①

Llanfoist

Monmouthshire & Brecon Canal

Hill's Tramroad

Rhiw Ifor

Walk 19

Walk 19

Cefn y Galchen

Foxhunter

N

0   Miles   ½

ficult. The ironmasters preferred to use the cheaper canal route to the world's busiest port at Newport. So Hill built a tunnel from Blaenavon, emerging on the northern side of the Blorenge. The tramroad then contoured round the side of the hill. It ended at a winch where a series of three inclines lowered cargo to the wharf on the canal at Llanfoist. TURN RIGHT and follow the course of the tramroad round the head of Cwm Siencyn, stepping across the stream. Continue along this easy and spectacular terrace as it contours the hillside. After a while you come to some industrial remains, the relics of the Garnddyrys forges that turned rough pig iron into a more useable product. You come to a track curving up from the valley. FOLLOW THIS TO THE RIGHT until it joins the main road.

5 TURN LEFT and walk carefully down the main road. Just after a right hand bend, BEAR RIGHT following the footpath sign to Llanfoist. This rejoins Hill's Tramroad just below a fence. The tramroad continues to contour around the mountain now with views right up the Usk valley. *Just above a wood you can see some more stone sleepers embedded in the path. As the path curves round onto the northern side of the Blorenge you pass the remains of a tunnel. This was probably built to protect the track from subsidence in the mountain.* Eventually the path, now narrower, curves round into the hollow of Cwm Craf. *This was the site of the winch house where the tram road ended at the top of the upper incline.* Where the fence turns down hill BRANCH LEFT to follow it to the field gate, where you rejoin your outward route at point **2**. Descend on the site of the inclines back to Llanfoist and the starting point.

AROUND THE BLORENGE

DESCRIPTION An easy walk to the summit of the Blorenge is followed by an exhilarating tour round the edge of the summit plateau. There are good tracks for the whole length of this 3½-mile jaunt that commands extensive views from Somerset to Mid Wales. There is hardly any climbing, a perfect mountain for those who like summits but hate the ascent! However there are glimpses of history all around, and you will enjoy spectacular views throughout.

START Pen-ffordd-goch Pond (better known locally as the Keeper's Pond). SO 254107.

DIRECTIONS The Keeper's Pond lies at the highest point on the B4246 between Blaenavon and Abergavenny. It is easily reached from either town. From Abergavenny follow signs through Llanfoist and climb up the steep hill via the double bends known as the 'Devil's Elbow'. There is a car park and other roadside parking places.

The nearby town of Blaenavon was declared a world heritage site in 2000, one of only about 20 such locations in Britain. The town played a pivotal role in the early development of iron production. The Blorenge is riddled with important archaeological remains and this area can rightly lay claim to be the cradle of the industrial revolution in Wales. Alexander Cordell's historical novel, 'Rape of the Fair Country', is set in nineteenth century industrial Monmouthshire and features many places in and around this walk and **Walk 18.** *In Blaenavon you can visit the old ironworks, now in the care of Cadw. The site includes ironworkers' cottages. Also in Blaenavon the national coal mining museum of Wales, 'Big Pit', offers trips underground. There is also a preserved steam railway, running on part of the line that served the upper reaches of the Eastern Valley. A number of second hand bookshops have opened in the town in an attempt to emulate the success of Hay-on-Wye.*

I Start from the car park, take time to look at the interpretation panel. *The pool was constructed to supply water to the forges at Garnddyrys further down the road towards Abergavenny and visited on* **Walk 18.** *The official name of the pond, Pen-ffordd-goch, means top of the red road, and may refer to the original road from Abergavenny to Blaenavon built in 1835. It was probably constructed from local red sandstone.* Follow the minor road eastwards in the direction of Llanellen until you reach the masts situated at the highest point on this road. There is another car park here.

2 TURN INTO THE CAR PARK. A track leads from the far side of this car park and heads directly for the summit of Blorenge. *Nearby is the Foxhunter memorial, remembering the horse which won the Olympic show jumping contest in 1948. There is a very gentle gradient but the track is quite stony. There are good views east towards over the valley of the Usk towards the Forest of Dean and the Cotswolds beyond.*

3 The summit itself is 559 metres above sea level and is marked by shattered rocks and a cairn. There is evidence of a bronze-age burial site here. The path continues beyond the summit across the plateau. Soon after the beginning of the descent from this plateau, it reaches a patch of hummocky ground with short grass, evidence of old workings. A brick shed stands right on the edge of the escarpment and there are magnificent views once again, this time northwards towards the Skirrid and beyond.

4 At the hut TURN SHARP LEFT, almost doubling back in fact, to follow a grassy path which leads just below the edge of the scarp and contours round the side of the mountain. *It offers an ever-changing panorama as it does so. Rounding the northern edge of the summit plateau, the path drops slightly and the prospect is north-west up the Usk valley. Further evidence of old quarry workings and an old tramway are passed.*

5 Later our path is joined from the right by the bridleway from Llanfoist. *This leads back down to join the Blorenge's most famous tramway, Hill's Tramroad, which lies further down the slope to your right. This took iron from Blaenavon, through a tunnel, contoured around the Blorenge leading to* the top of an incline. The incline was used to take goods from the tramroad down to the canal wharf at Llanfoist, from where they could be taken by barge to Newport. KEEP STRAIGHT AHEAD. This walk heads directly back to the car park along the clear track.

The Blorenge

THE SKIRRID

DESCRIPTION At 3 miles this is a short, but rewarding, walk up the most easterly outlier of the Black Mountains. Its distinctive silhouette and its legendary status give the Skirrid an appeal and reputation far beyond its modest 486-metre elevation. The Skirrid, or more properly Ysgyryd Fawr, is one of the three peaks dominating the approaches to Abergavenny, the other two being the Blorenge and the Sugar Loaf. (The lesser-known Ysgyryd Fach is a wooded hill immediately east of Abergavenny.) The path climbs the wooded southern slopes before traversing the long, airy ridge, which offers all round views across the region. A return route threads its way around the eastern side of the mountain.

START Car park on the B4521, about two miles east of Abergavenny. SO 328164.

DIRECTIONS The car park is easily reached on B4521, which runs from Abergavenny to Ross via Skenfrith.

I From the car park a sign-posted, stone dressed, footpath leads uphill between two hedges. *The National Trust has owned the Skirrid since 1939 so there is a long history of access. The paths and car park are well maintained and it would be very hard to get lost. This walk has several particular attractions. First, it offers a sense of achievement and excellent views without the need for a major mountaineering expedition. The path up is clear, firm and well drained. So it might be good option for young children who would enjoy a challenge but not a route march. Secondly, it's quite short, so it's a viable walk if you have limited time, such as on a summer evening. Finally, it abounds in interest, offering tales and legends, and a variety of woodland and heathland habitats. The lower slopes benefit from extensive shade on a hot day.* At the top of the approach path a stile leads on to the thickly wooded hillside. Shortly after this the footpath diverges to the RIGHT off the main track and climbs some steps up through the woods. Yellow arrows confirm your choice. Keep ascending the well-engineered, waymarked track up through the woods, ignoring any tracks that cross it, until you reach a gate. Pass through this and turn RIGHT to continue your ascent up the clear path through woodland. *Rudolf Hess, Hitler's deputy, was captured after landing in Britain during the war. He often walked on the Skirrid while being held as a prisoner of war in nearby Maindiff Court.* Soon some steps and a stone built footpath lead steeply out of the woods into open heath land. The path now leads along the crest of a narrow, airy, but quite safe ridge. *Views extend west across the Black Mountains and east across the rich fertile farmland of north Monmouthshire to the Forest of Dean. This land has been fought over through history and is dotted with castles bearing testimony to conflict. White Castle, for example, is in view about three miles to the south-east. The ridge offers an easy, fairly level walk, with an occasional steeper section. Just before the summit, a few mounds and stones are evidence of the remains of St Michael's Chapel. Two upright stones mark the doorway and the foundations can also be traced. The history of this chapel is unclear but it is certainly very ancient. Arnold's 'Examinations as to Popery' in 1660 says that 'a hundred papists meet on the top of a high hill in Monmouthshire, called St Michael's Mount, where there is a ruinous chapel and a stone with crosses on it'.*

2 A National Trust trig point marks the highest point where the ground drops steeply away to the north. *Steep rocky cliffs buttress the summit of Ysgyryd Fawr and a strange looking landslip lies to the west of the summit. There are many legends about the landslip and the Skirrid's strange shape. The best-known story alleges that the mountain was rent in two at the time of Christ's crucifixion. The Skirrid is also known locally as St Michael's Mount and as the Holy Mountain. Farmers were known to collect soil from its slopes to cure ailing cattle. In fact, the landslip occurred at the time of the last ice age. Many people choose to return by the same route and enjoy the open promenade along the summit ridge with views in the opposite direction. However, you can* make a circular walk by retracing your steps about 300 yards just as far as the hummocks. Here turn SHARP LEFT to find a path that descends diagonally through the bracken. It becomes increasingly distinct as it drops down the hillside.

3 A fence marks the boundary of the National Trust land at the bottom. Just short of this, turn RIGHT to follow a way through the ubiquitous bracken. This path contours round the base of Ysgyryd Fawr but is sufficiently high above the countryside to the east to offer good views. Eventually the path curves round the side of the hill, through the woods and rejoins the main path. Follow your original route back to the start.

Ysgyryd Fawr

Just in case...

If you are undertaking a high-level walk, regardless of the time of year, you need to be properly equipped. Welsh weather is often fickle, and what begins as a fine day can finish with rain, or snow, or mist, or wind. So take a comfortable and waterproof rucksack (or line it with a plastic sack) and *ensure you use, or have with you,* the following basic gear at all times:

- waterproof jacket with a hood, and waterproof trousers
- walking boots (with gaiters if you wish)
- warm and comfortable socks, and a hat
- light but warm sweater and trousers
- windproof gloves or mittens
- high energy food, and water

- a map, pencil and compass
- basic first aid kit
- Swiss Army Knife or multi-tool
- *and you can add any comfort items, plus a camera, mobile phone (fully charged!), sunglasses and so on as you wish (but keep your rucksack as light as possible)*

KEY TO THE MAPS

——— Main road

——— Minor road

●▬►▬● Walk route & direction

(1) Walk instruction

– – – Adjoining path

∿ River or stream

G Gate

S Stile

△ Summit

🌲🌳 Woods or forest

🍺 Pub

P Parking

THE COUNTRYSIDE CODE

- Be safe – plan ahead and follow any signs

- Leave gates and property as you find them

- Protect plants and animals, and take your litter home

- Keep dogs under close control

- Consider other people

The CroW Act 2000, implemented throughout Wales in May 2005, introduced new legal rights of access for walkers to designated open country, predominantly mountain, moor, heath or down, plus all registered common land. This access can be subject to restrictions and closure for land management or safety reasons for up to 28 days a year.

Published by
Kittiwake
3 Glantwymyn Village Workshops, Glantwymyn, Machynlleth, Montgomeryshire SY20 8LY

© Text: Alastair Ross 2006
© Maps & illustrations: Kittiwake 2006
Drawings by Morag Perrott
Cover photographs by Alastair Ross:
large: The Grwyne Fechan Valley, from Walk 15 :
inset: Llanthony Priory, Walks 3, 4 & 7.

Care has been taken to be accurate.
However neither the author nor the publisher can accept responsibility for any errors which may appear, or their consequences. If you are in any doubt about access, check before you proceed.

Printed by MWL, Pontypool.

Revised edition 2007. Reprinted twice 2007.
Minor revisions 2008. Reprinted twice 2009.
ISBN: **978 1 902302 41 6**